Gene Therapy: Medicine's New Frontier

Gene Therapy: Medicine's New Frontier

Written by: Mariyam Sardar, Mohathir Sheikh, Margarita Liubetskaya, Darla Chloe Daniva, Cassandra Van Drunen, Angelin Valancia Thipahar, Sahir Dhalla, Austin Mardon, Catherine Mardon

Edited by: Kanish Baskaran & Naiya Patel

Designed by: Josh Kramer

Published by Golden Meteorite Press
2021

Gene Therapy: Medicine's New Frontier
Copyright © 2021 by Austin Mardon
All rights reserved.

This book or any portion thereof may not be reproduced or used in any manner whatsoever without the express written permission of the publisher except for the use of brief quotations in a review.

First Printing: 2021

ISBN: 978-1-77369-622-5

Golden Meteorite Press
103 11919 82 St NW
Edmonton, AB T5B 2W3
www.goldenmeteoritepress.com
aamardon@yahoo.ca
Alberta, Canada

Table of Contents

Chapter 1: What Is Gene Therapy?	1
Chapter 2: History/Background	11
Chapter 3: Discovery of Gene Therapy	19
Chapter 4: Gene Doping	31
Chapter 5: Clinical Applications of Gene Therapy	39
Chapter 6: Social and Ethical Concerns of Gene Therapy	47
Chapter 7: Future Directions of Gene Therapy	57

Introduction

Gene Therapy describes an experimental technique that uses genes to treat or prevent genetic disease. The technology has the potential to revolutionize the treatment of a wide variety of genetic conditions, from cancer to heart disease, and recent technological leaps have accelerated its research and adoption. This book delves into the topic of Gene Therapy, including its history and discovery, clinical applications, ethical concerns and impact on society.

Chapter 1: What Is Gene Therapy?

Mariam Sardar

Introduction

Gene therapy is becoming widely available due to new advances in genetics and bioengineering (Rangel Gonçalves & de Melo Alves Paiva, 2017). From finding the inheritance pattern to discovering the technique to isolate the genes have led to the discovery of gene therapy. The gene therapy has demonstrated immense success in genetic diseases, such as cystic fibrosis, hemophilia, Leber congenital amaurosis, muscular dystrophy, sickle cell anemia, ornithine transcarbamylase deficiency, Pompe disease, Gaucher's disease, cancer, combined immunodeficiency syndrome, and certain viral infections (Rangel Gonçalves & de Melo Alves Paiva, 2017; Scheller & Krebsbach, 2009; Cotrim & Baum, 2008). This chapter aims to discuss the definition of gene therapy, the origin of gene therapy, the process of gene therapy, types of vectors and types of gene therapy, an overview of clinical application of gene therapy and its challenges, problems of gene therapy, and lastly, the future of gene therapy.

What is Gene Therapy?

Gene therapy is a process of inserting foreign DNA into the human genome to replace the mutated gene with a healthy gene (Rangel Gonçalves & de Melo Alves Paiva, 2017; Scheller & Krebsbach, 2009; Carmichael, 2014; Cotrim & Baum, 2008; Dickler and Collier, 1994; Wirth et al., 2013; Food and Drug Administration [FDA], 2017). Gene therapy is performed when no other possible treatments are available. It attempts to treat, cure or minimize the effects of the disease (Rangel Gonçalves & de Melo Alves Paiva, 2017). Gene therapy exists mainly in research labs, and its application has been experimental to date (Rangel Gonçalves & de Melo Alves Paiva, 2017). A stem of gene therapy is gene doping (Pray, 2008). Gene doping is a similar process to gene therapy (Pray, 2008). One significant difference is that the insertion of a gene aims to enhance the functional property of a normal gene (Pray, 2008). Experiments for gene therapy have exceptionally been performed in counties like the United States, Europe, Australia, and China (Rangel Gonçalves & de Melo Alves Paiva, 2017). The diseases that are mainly researched for treatments using gene therapy are recessive gene disorder, acquired genetic diseases, and some viral infections such as AIDS (Rangel Gonçalves & de Melo Alves Paiva, 2017). There are risks associated with gene therapy as the technique itself is very complicated.

History of Gene Therapy

The notion of genome inheritance originated from ancient Greek, and this theory persisted from then with no evidence (Rangel Gonçalves & de Melo Alves Paiva, 2017). In the early 1850s, genetic studies were conducted to prove the theory (Rangel Gonçalves & de Melo Alves Paiva, 2017). In 1850, Gregor Mendel, who is now known as the father of inheritance, discovered the inheritance pattern by experimenting with peas (Rangel Gonçalves & de Melo Alves Paiva, 2017). Another discovery that contributed to gene therapy is Frederick Griffith's experiment in 1928 (Wirth et al., 2013). His experiments with rats revealed the transforming principle: the ability to transfer genetic information (Wirth et al., 2013). In 1950, James Watson and Francis Crick uncovered the structure of the double-strand DNA (Rangel Gonçalves & de Melo Alves Paiva, 2017). In 1970, researchers discovered restriction enzymes that initiated splicing in specific locations (Rangel Gonçalves & de Melo Alves Paiva, 2017). Gene splicing is a process where genes are separated and reinserted (Rangel Gonçalves & de Melo Alves Paiva, 2017). The discovery of restriction enzymes has led to the progression of genetic engineering (Rangel Gonçalves & de Melo Alves Paiva, 2017). Since then, new drugs and antibodies have been manufactured (Rangel Gonçalves & de Melo Alves Paiva, 2017). Around the same time, Jonathan Beckwith discovered the process of isolating a single genome from an entire genome (Carmichael, 2014). By 1980, the concept of gene therapy was introduced and is still extensively researched for new treatments (Rangel Gonçalves & de Melo Alves Paiva, 2017).

Vectors

Before discussing the process of gene therapy, it is important to understand the vectors. Vectors are transporter mechanisms that store the healthy genetic sequence and release the genetic sequence when the vectors are inserted into the targeted cell (Rangel Gonçalves & de Melo Alves Paiva, 2017; Scheller & Krebsbach, 2009; Cotrim & Baum, 2008; Dickler and Collier, 1994; Wirth et al., 2013). There are two types of vectors - viral and non-viral (Cotrim & Baum, 2008). Insertion of genes through viral transduction is the most common application in gene therapy (Scheller & Krebsbach, 2009) because of their ability to invade cells and insert their DNA into the host cell (Rangel Gonçalves & de Melo Alves Paiva, 2017). Viral vectors are used in almost 70% of the trials (Cotrim and Baum, 2008). Some of the viruses that are used as vectors are retrovirus, adenovirus, lentivirus, herpes simplex virus, and adeno-associated virus (Rangel Gonçalves & de Melo Alves Paiva, 2017; Scheller & Krebsbach, 2009; Cotrim and Baum, 2008). Usually, the viruses are disease-causing; however, these viruses are modified and are not pathogenic (FDA, 2017). Aside from viral vectors, other vectors are liposomes, plasmids, and polymers (Scheller & Krebsbach, 2009). A type of non-viral gene delivery is polymeric gene delivery, which contains two kinds of polymers: synthetic and natural polymer (Scheller & Krebsbach, 2009). Some of the natural polymers that are used as vectors are cyclodextrin, chitosan, collagen, gelatin, and alginate (Scheller & Krebsbach, 2009).

Process of Gene Therapy

A technique that is often used for gene therapy is recombinant DNA technology (Rangel Gonçalves & de Melo Alves Paiva, 2017). In this technique, the healthy gene is inserted into a vector, such as plasmodial, nanostructured, or viral (Rangel Gonçalves & de Melo Alves Paiva, 2017). Next, this vector is inserted into the targeted cells (FDA, 2017). Another way of inserting the vector is by taking the patient's part of the tissue, and then the cells are separated in the lab (FDA, 2017). The vector is then injected into the cell in the lab (FDA, 2017). Cells are left to multiply, and then the cells are injected back into the body(FDA, 2017). The healthy gene replicates to have a functional protein (FDA, 2017).

Types of Gene Therapy

The two types of targeted cells are germline cells and somatic cells (Rangel Gonçalves & de Melo Alves Paiva, 2017). In germline-cell gene therapy, the sperm or egg are altered with the insertion of healthy genes (Rangel Gonçalves & de Melo Alves Paiva, 2017). This type of therapy is hereditary, which intends to be inherited by the following generations (Rangel Gonçalves & de Melo Alves Paiva, 2017). Gene therapy of germline cells can theoretically treat genetic and hereditary diseases (Rangel Gonçalves & de Melo Alves Paiva, 2017). Somatic-cell gene therapy alters the DNA of the somatic cells, which are any bodily cells except the sperm and egg (Rangel Gonçalves & de Melo Alves Paiva, 2017). This type of therapy only affects the person on whom the gene therapy is performed (Rangel Gonçalves & de Melo Alves Paiva, 2017).

Application of Gene Therapy

In January of 1989, the first clinical application of gene therapy was approved by the National Institutes of Health (Scheller & Krebsbach, 2009). In the September of 1990, the approved gene therapy was performed on a four-year-old girl battling a severe combined immunodeficiency (SCID) (Scheller & Krebsbach, 2009). The treatment was successful, and she continued to live her life (Scheller & Krebsbach, 2009). For the following decade, gene therapy was performed on approximately 3000 people (Scheller & Krebsbach, 2009).

Over the years, many complications in patients have occurred. One of the cases was of an 18-year old who died after four days of the insertion of adenovirus in his liver (Scheller & Krebsbach, 2009). Hence, more precautions to clinical trials and new techniques are required. Despite some failures in gene therapy, this therapy is a promising treatment in the future (Scheller & Krebsbach, 2009).

Some factors are considered before performing human gene therapy trials (Dickler & Collier, 1994). First, the sequence of the gene must be known of the disease by cloning the disease gene. Second, the functional properties of the normal and abnormal genes must be determined before the process can occur (Scheller & Krebsbach, 2009). Third, the insertion of the gene should be tested in vitro (Scheller & Krebsbach, 2009). Lastly, if feasible and ethical, experiment the gene therapy in an animal model (Scheller & Krebsbach, 2009). For instance, a six-year-old boy was diagnosed with a genetic disease called Leber congenital amaurosis type 2, LCA2 (Carmichael, 2014). In LCA2 disease, the enzyme RPE65 is missing (Carmichael, 2014). In 1988, a veterinarian discovered that dogs with impaired vision also have the same faulty gene (Carmichael, 2014). The discovery led to the clinical trials of gene therapy on blinds Briards (Carmichael, 2014). In a few days, the dogs regained their vision (Carmichael, 2014). Due to the success of the trial, a similar procedure was performed on the six-year-old boy, which was a success (Carmichael, 2014).

Challenges of Gene Therapy

It is still experimental because gene therapy is very challenging and complex. For example, some of the challenges of gene therapy are: mutated cells must be accessible for treatment and insertion of healthy genes; an effective technique is required to distribute gene copies to the cells; the formation of the disease and its structure (genetic bonds) must be thoroughly understood; last but not least, the two types of targeted cells makes the gene therapy more complicated (Rangel Gonçalves & de Melo Alves Paiva, 2017). The process of releasing the healthy gene into targeted cells is complicated and requires precision due to various challenges. Some of the obstacles are releasing the gene to a specific location of the cell, going undetected by the immune system, ability to produce in larger quantities, and no allergic reactions or inflammation must occur after the vector is inserted (Rangel Gonçalves & de Melo Alves Paiva, 2017).

Concerns with Gene Therapy

As reported before, the death of an 18-year-old male in September 1999 has led to a major setback for gene therapy (Carmichael, 2014; Cotrim & Baum, 2008). It was reported that the 18-year-old male died due to an immune reaction to the vector, adenovirus (Cotrim & Baum, 2008). After this case, the clinical trials were halted. The Food and Drug Administration (FDA) investigated the case, finding that the clinical trials had not taken proper safety measures (Cotrim & Baum, 2008). After five years of FDA investigation, the gene therapy experiments are now closely regulated by NIH and FDA (Cotrim & Baum, 2008). An ethical issue that was raised was the modification of germ cells. Although somatic gene therapy is generally accepted, the modification of germ cells is disapproved to a great extent (Rangel Gonçalves & de Melo Alves Paiva, 2017). It is morally questioned whether or not it is acceptable to alter an inheritance genome (Rangel Gonçalves & de Melo Alves Paiva, 2017).

Current and Future of Gene Therapy

Most of the clinical trials on gene therapy are currently for treating cancer (Wirth et al., 2013). 60% of the gene therapy trials are cancer-related (Wirth et al., 2013). The second most clinical trials are on monogenetic and cardiovascular diseases (Wirth et al., 2013). As of 2013, more than 1800 clinical trials for gene therapy are approved worldwide and are currently in progress (Wirth et al., 2013). The vectors that are commonly used are naked plasmid DNA, retroviral and adenoviral vectors (Wirth et al., 2013).

A member of NIH, Dr. Michael Gottesman, examined the prospects of gene therapy (Dickler & Collier, 1994). The human genome project and his work from his lab focus on developing a " dominant selectable marker" (Dickler & Collier, 1994). The project's goal is to have a complete DNA sequence of the human genome to understand the human body and the related diseases (Dickler & Collier, 1994). The increasing efforts to have a complete DNA sequence of the human genome have led to the possibility of isolating the genes that are associated with more than 4000 human genetic diseases (Dickler & Collier, 1994). A technique that has led to this discovery is positional cloning (Dickler & Collier, 1994). The positioning cloning has aided in isolating genes for diseases such as CF, Duchenne's muscular dystrophy, and Hungtington's disease (Dickler & Collier, 1994). This technique is promising and will enable the identification of more DNA markers (Dickler & Collier, 1994).

Conclusion

With more research, gene therapy will be a promising treatment for various diseases. Gene therapy is a solution to the resistance to current drugs or antibiotics. As per the clinical trials of gene therapy, gene therapy has cured many patients that were not curable with drugs. For example, the six-year-old boy who was suffering from LCA2 (Carmichael, 2014). LCA2 is not curable with drugs, but gene therapy has a promising treatment for LCA2 (Carmichael, 2014). Despite the successful clinical trials, gene therapy is surrounded with skepticism due to some failures and risks associated with gene therapy. Gene therapy is very complicated and complex. For a successful gene therapy treatment, from the choice of vector to the type of target and insertion of the vector, all is needed to be considered. Hence, gene therapy is still in the process of clinical trials. New advances and techniques are required for minimal risks in gene therapy. In the future, gene therapy will not be a treatment but a cure for many diseases that are not curable currently with drugs.

Chapter 2: History/Background

Mohathir Shiekh

Introduction

Gene therapy has started to make some serious progress in recent years and is poised to have a significant impact on the practice of medicine in treating diseases (Scollay, 2001). There are now more than 1700 approved clinical trials globally since the initial gene therapy trials were conducted two decades ago (Wirth et al., 2013). Gene therapy is an experimental technique that uses genes to treat or prevent disease (What is gene therapy, 2021). There are several approaches researchers can use including:

- Introducing a new gene into the body to fight the disease
- Replacing a mutated, diseases causing gene with a healthy copy of the gene
- Inactivating or "knocking out" a mutated gene that is functioning improperly

However, in the past, most gene therapy trials were unsuccessful with only 1% of them reaching phase three, but none going any further (Scollay, 2001). The first death linked to gene therapy drew greater public attention and exposed several clinical studies with inadequate ethical standards and trial designs. Unfortunately, these revelations cast a shadow on the field of gene therapy and lingering concerns still exist. Despite these setbacks, success stories are developing from recent trials and the knowledge and information gained from these studies are helping advance the field of gene therapy (Wirth et al., 2013).

History

The concept of gene therapy first arose in the 1960s and early 1970s during the development of genetically marked cell lines to understand the mechanism of cell transformation by the papovaviruses: polyoma and SV40 (Friedmann, 1992). These cell lines were used to test the notion that foreign DNA could be introduced permanently, stably, functionally, and heritably into mammalian cells to provide permanent new genetic functions. Conceptually, the studies were derived from the Avery, McLeod, and McCarthy studies of DNA-mediated genetic transformation of pneumococci. Before the papovavirus studies, researchers were focused on the purine salvage pathway enzyme called hypoxanthine-guanine phosphoribosyltransferase (HPRT). Researchers were able to chemically select cells expressing this enzyme and focused on transferring this gene into rodent cell lines that were HPRT deficient. These early studies were able to demonstrate that mammalian cells could be incorporated with foreign DNA and could even express the transferred genes. However, these early methods were extremely inefficient, generally did not result in stable expression of the foreign genetic material, and could not be reproduced consistently. The papovavirus studies found the papovaviruses SV40 and polyoma were able to integrate their genetic information stably and heritably into the genome of target cells. It also became evident that portions of the transferred viral genome could remain expressed in the transformed cells.

This was an important observation as researchers started to hypothesize if other viruses could be modified to carry potentially therapeutic foreign genes instead of their native genes into defective cells. However, this was before the development of recombinant DNA and researchers had to envision other ways to incorporate and express foreign genes. In the late 1960s, researchers injected wild-type Shope papillomavirus into two young girls suffering from hyperargininemia, in the hopes the viral genome would encode an arginase that could be incorporated and expressed in the host. Unfortunately, the destination cells were poorly defined and the biochemical and virological foundation of the experiment was incorrect, resulting in the experiment failing with little to no useful information being obtained.

Between 1966 to 1970 there was an increase in discussions surrounding public policy and ethical issues in the potential application of genetics to human diseases. In the early 1970s, reports started to appear that hinted that the recombinant DNA era would provide the tools necessary for human gene therapy. The two tools were specific genes in cloned form and an efficient method of gene transfer. In 1970, researchers discovered enzymes responsible for the separation and reinsertion of genes along the DNA molecule (Gonçalves & Paiva, 2017). Most importantly these enzymes were able to function in a reproducible manner. In the following years, researchers learned more about the mechanism of infection and transcription by RNA tumour viruses (Friedmann, 1992). In 1973 a new calcium phosphate transfection method was developed. The human beta-globin gene was one of the early targets for gene transfer and gene therapy studies due to its relevance to human disease. As a result, the human beta-globin gene was one the earliest genes to be successfully cloned. Using the new calcium phosphate transfection method, studies were able to demonstrate the introduction of the human beta-globin gene into mammalian cells efficiently and functionally. The calcium phosphate transfection method was also able to introduce other cloned genes and, in some cases, total cellular DNA into mammalian cells.

The Cline Experiments

In 1980, Martin Cline, the head of the UCLA hematology division, conducted a human gene transfer experiment that would have a drastic effect on the field of human gene therapy (Beutler, 2001). Martin Cline was a highly respected biomedical scientist and had a distinguished and productive career in clinical medicine and basic science research. He initiated one of the early bone marrow transplantation programs at UCLA and his experience with hematopoietic stem cells and gene transfer technology made him uniquely qualified to perform human gene transfer studies focused on the genetic disease of hematopoiesis. Martin Cline and his colleagues at UCLA reported that they could introduce the human beta-globin gene into rodent bone marrow cells using calcium phosphate transfection (Friedmann, 1992). The team claimed the genetically modified bone marrow cells were partially successful in repopulating the marrow of the irradiated recipient rodents. Despite the surprising findings of this experiment due to the known inefficiency of the transfection method, the findings helped spur Cline to proceed with the human gene transfer experiment. The human gene transfer experiment had two patients, both with severe beta thalassemia (Beutler, 2001). The patient's bone marrow cells were transfected in vitro with a plasmid containing

human beta-globin gene and then re-infused into the patients after a segment of their femur was irradiated (Beutler, 2001; Friedmann, 1992). The experiment had no clinical benefit to the patients and other researchers found it difficult to accept the transfected viral sequences that were detected in the peripheral blood of the patients for up to 10 weeks after the re-infusion due to the detection method used in the experiment (Beutler, 2001). After the experiment was conducted it was revealed that Cline did not have approval from the UCLA Institutional Review Board to run human trials (Beutler, 2001; Friedmann, 1992). Despite permission being obtained in Jerusalem and Naples where the studies were conducted, the protocol was modified after gaining permission (Beutler, 2001). This resulted in Cline losing his chair at UCLA and his research funding (Friedmann, 1992). Further complicating the issue was the lack of positive evidence that the rodent experiments, which spurred on the human experiments, were successful in creating the response reported by Cline and his colleagues (Beutler, 2001). Luckily the patients were not harmed; however, the existing fear and uncertainty surrounding gene therapy experiments played a large role in how the community reacted to Cline's experiment.
The study for the most part catalyzed the science, ethics, and public policy aspects in this field of research (Beutler, 2001; Friedmann, 1992). The Recombinant DNA Advisory Committee of the NIH, which regulates recombinant DNA studies, established a Gene Therapy Subcommittee to specifically regulate molecular genetic techniques and tools to human use (Friedmann, 1992). This change made the potential use of recombinant DNA for human gene therapy extremely visible and broadened its outreach to the general human genetic, molecular genetic, and medical communities.

Development of Retroviral Vectors

Until now, all the previous gene transfer tools used in experiments were inefficient and it was difficult to create reproducible results using those tools. Back in 1970 researchers had discovered integrated DNA copies of the viral RNA genome in infected cells, but their potential use in gene therapy only became evident in the 1980s. By 1981, the transduction capabilities and life cycle of the retroviruses were well understood and their potential as a gene transfer tool was starting to be recognized. Studies conducted in 1981 and 1982 reported techniques that allowed retroviruses to combine their genetic information with other retroviruses to create highly efficient vectors, which displayed the ability to infect almost 100% of exposed human and other mammalian cells. Additional studies found and developed efficient helper cell lines, which are packaging cells that are capable of producing retrovirus vectors with high efficiency (Koo, 2014). In 1983, the clinical and molecular biology communities came together effectively to stress the rigor and caution of using retroviral vectors in relevant experiments. This meeting highlighted the shift in the community from questioning if human gene therapy could be developed but rather when and how it will be developed. In the same year, retroviral vectors were used to correct disease phenotypes in vitro in human disease cells (Friedmann, 1992). As mentioned earlier, the HPRT experiments conducted before the 1960s were successful in demonstrating the transfer of genetic material as possible, but the experiments were unsuccessful in correcting the HPRT deficiency in the cells. With the use of HPRT retroviral vectors, researchers were able to restore HPRT enzyme expression to the HPRT deficient cells. The restored HPRT function in the cells also corrected the defects in the cells caused by the previously missing enzyme. Two years later, a similar result was seen when treating adenosine deaminase (ADA) deficiency in severe combined immunodeficiency disease (SCID). The ADA retroviral vectors restored ADA expression in the SCID patient cells and corrected the cell sensitivity to the toxic effects of accumulated deoxyadenosine. At this point, many different studies started to come out displaying genetic diseases and their cell types that are susceptible to genetic modification with retroviral vectors including:

- Fibroblasts
- Bone marrow stem and progenitor cells
- Hepatocytes
- Keratinocytes
- Skeletal muscle myoblasts
- Vascular endothelial cells
- Airway epithelial cells

Human Trials

The first human gene therapy trial was conducted in 1990 (Friedmann, 1992; Mitha, 2020). A four-year girl suffering from SCID underwent a 12-day treatment using ADA retroviral vector (Mitha, 2020). This experiment was a success with the treatment improving the patient immune system, allowing her to live a normal life. This was a major milestone and catalyzed multiple further trials throughout the 1990s. However, in 1999, the gene therapy field encountered a significant setback when an 18 year patient died during a gene therapy clinical trial at the University of Pennsylvania. This was the first reported death directly linked to gene therapy and it drew significant media attention. The US FDA suspended the university's entire gene therapy program and launched investigations into 69 other gene therapy trials occurring around the country. The investigation criticized many clinical trial designs and urged a slower and more cautious approach when administering the viral vectors to help increase the safety of the trials. The rebound of the gene therapy field has been slow but steady. In 2003, China was the first nation to officially approve a gene therapy called Gendicine which is used to treat head and neck cancer. China was followed by Russia when it approved Neovasculgen for the treatment of peripheral artery disease in 2012. With more gene therapy studies getting approved globally, the FDA expects the approval rate in the US to reach 10 to 20 cell and gene therapies per year by 2025.

In general, the early approach to gene therapy focused on targeting enzyme defects and deficiencies. Now with advances in technology and our understanding of gene transfer mechanisms of action, the gene therapy field has expanded to target more complex diseases. Huge gaps in knowledge surrounding virus biology, vector dynamics, immune interaction, and vector safety have been filled since the late 90s and early 2000s. With new approaches and techniques constantly being studied, gene therapy has come a long way since it was first conceptualized and continues to have enormous potential to change modern medicine in the future.

Chapter 3: Discovery of Gene Therapy

Margarita Liubetskaya

Introduction

Now that we touched base on what gene therapy is, its various processes, applications, and challenges, this chapter will take a closer look at the history, specifically the discovery of gene therapy. Chapter One gave a good introduction to the historical development of gene therapy by encompassing the notion of the genome, genetic studies, Gregor Mendel and inheritance, Fredrick Griffith and the transforming principle, the discovery of the double-helix structure of DNA, enzyme splicing, restriction enzymes, and the concept of isolating specific genes from an entire genome. This chapter will explore and go beyond some of these subjects. There will be a specific focus on popular and important names associated with gene therapy and its discovery, who those individuals were/are, and significant trials that contributed to its implementation.

The Transforming Principle

Frederick Griffith (1849-1914) was a British physician, pathologist, and bacteriologist. He first studied medicine at the University of Liverpool and later worked at the Pathological Laboratory of the Ministry of Health. In his studies, he focussed on the epidemiology and pathology of bacterial pneumonia and had a reputation for conducting thorough and methodical research (Britannica, T. Editors of Encyclopaedia, 2021).

In 1928, Griffith conducted research and published a report, "Griffith's Experiment", which explored two strains of the Streptococcus pneumoniae bacterium. The two strains were virulent and avirulent, the first meaning it was lethal to mice and the ladder, harmless. Griffith discovered that mice that were injected with either of the two strains remained infection-free, however, the mice that received a mixture of both became infected and died. He uncovered that some type of chemical, the "transforming principle", was able to transfer from dead virulent cells into virulent ones and change them. This is how the pneumococcus transformed from Type I to Type II (Wirth, Parker, and Ylä-Herttuala, 2013). Additionally, this transformation was heritable, meaning it can be passed down through generations. Griffith died in 1941 during a German bombing raid on London. He continues to live on in history as his work sparked further research which uncovered that the transforming substance he worked on was none other than the genetic material of the cell - deoxyribonucleic acid, DNA. This was done by Oswald Avery, Colin MacLeod, and Maclyn McCarty.

Deoxyribonucleic Acid

Oswald Avery (1877-1955) was a Canadian-American physician, medical researcher, bacteriologist, who received his degree from Columbia University College of Physicians and Surgeons. After initially spending some years in clinical practice, he became involved in bacteriological research at the Hoagland Laboratory. In 1913 he joined the staff of the Rockefeller Institute Hospital, where he began studying the bacterium responsible for lobar pneumonia, Streptococcus pneumoniae, called the pneumococcus, the kind that Griffith used to uncover the "transforming principle".

Colin MacLeod (1909-1972) was a Canadian-American physician and geneticist. He received his M.D. from McGill University. He completed his internship and in 1934, he moved to New York City and joined Avery at the Rockefeller Institute for Medical Research in his work with pneumococcus, first as an assistant and, later in 1938, as an actual associate.

The third member of the trio, Maclyn McCarty (1911-2005), was also a physician and a geneticist. McCarty attended Stanford (B.S.) and Johns Hopkins School of Medicine. After which he was introduced to the study of pneumococci bacteria and arranged to work with Avery by William S, Tillet. An interesting fact is that McCarty is described as "the last surviving member of the Manhattan scientific team that overturned medical dogma in the 1940s and became the first to demonstrate the genes were made of DNA". He worked at Rockefeller University "for more than 60 years" (Altman, 2005).

Together, these three men dramatically changed the understanding of the molecular basis of life. They uncovered while purifying the "transforming substance", discovered by Griffith, that the transformation observed was deoxyribonucleic acid, not protein, as previously suspected by the larger scientific population. Thus, Avery, Macleod, and McCarty shifted the world of genetics and DNA became the topic of interest and sparked the next generation of discoverers as seen in the above picture of McCarty with Crick and Watson, whose contribution we will cover later on in this chapter.

Conjugation and Transduction

Joshua Lederberg (1925-2008) was an American geneticist and labeled as a "pioneer" in his field. He studied at Yale under Edward Tatum and together they discovered that certain bacteria were able to transfer genetic material by mating, and so conjugation was born (Tatum and Lederberg, 1947). Later, this time with Norton Zinder, Lederberg discovered a third mechanism of transfer, transduction (Zinder and Lederberg, 1952). Together, Lederberg and Zinder observed that recombination of genetic material could occur even through a fine glass filter and initially suspected "active filtrate" to be the cause, however, later discovered that bacteriophage was responsible for this. This bacteriophage is what carries DNA from one bacterium to another. The name "transduction" is meant to represent the mechanism of this process. This discovery was crucial for our gene therapy timeline but also the scientific community beyond it. The process explained how "bacteria of different species could gain resistance to the same antibiotic very quickly" (Wirth, Parker, and Ylä-Herttuala, 2013). This initiated the exploration of potential benefits of this process for eukaryotic, animal, cells.

The Double-Helix of DNA

The discovery of the double-helix structure of DNA is a controversial subject in the science world. As of recent evidence, it has been suggested that the previous discoverers of the phenomena may not have given full credit where credit is due to one of the larger contributors.

James Watson (born 1928) is an American biologist, geneticist, and zoologist. He and his partner, Francis Crick (1916-2004), a British molecular biologist, biophysicist, and neuroscientist, are largely credited for the discovery of the double-helical structure of DNA in 1953, which suggested and supported the idea of a possible copying mechanism for genetic material. This was a key discovery for the development of gene therapy (Bansal, 2003).

Rosalind Franklin (1920-1958) was an English chemist and X-ray crystallographer. She provided crucial clues and evidence to the structure of DNA and proved and confirmed the Watson-Crick DNA model. Watson and Crick, although not in contact with Franklyn directly, used her x-ray diffraction photos of viruses. Crick admitted that based on her images, Franklyn was "two steps away" from discovering the correct structure of the spring herself, and Watson was contradicted and criticized by many colleagues and challenged for his ill-representation of Franklyn.

Franklyn was diagnosed with ovarian cancer in 1956 and died at age 37 in 1958. She never received recognition for the work she had done until after her death, however, was on good terms, even friendly, with both Watson and Crick when she had passed. She died proud of her work and her world reputation in the research world (Maddox, 2003), regardless of not winning a Nobel Peace Prize for her contribution.

> *"Science and everyday life cannot and should not be separated. Science, for me, gives a partial explanation of life. In so far as it goes, it is based on fact, experience, and experiment. . . . I agree that faith is essential to success in life, but I do not accept your definition of faith, i.e., belief in life after death. In my view, all that is necessary for faith is the belief that by doing our best we shall come nearer to success and that success in our aims (the improvement of the lot of mankind, present and future) is worth attaining."*
> *– Rosalind Franklin in a letter to Ellis Franklin, ca. summer 1940 ("Biographical Overview", n.d.)*

Viruses

Howard Temin (1934-1994) was an American geneticist and virologist. While in high school, Temin participated in the Jackson Laboratory's Summer Student Program where his director referred to him as "unquestionably the finest scientist of the fifty-seven students who have attended the program since the beginning..." the director told Temin's parents, "I can't help but feel this boy is destined to become a really great man in the field of science.", which was quite the prophecy and could not have become more accurate (Harman, Dietrich, and Dietrich, 2009). After his studies in 1961, a decade after phages were found to be capable of transferring genetic material from one bacterium to another, Temin discovered that similarly, specific genetic mutations could be inherited through virus infections. This paved the way for gene therapy as it uncovered that genetic information could flow from RNA to DNA and this led to the discovery of RNA-dependent DNA polymerase. Also, through this, it was uncovered that the acquisition of a new characteristic was inherited through the chromosomal insertion of foreign genetic material (Sambrook et al., 1968).

The importance of viruses became more and more apparent and as the amount of cell transformation studies surged, genetic engineering became a possible new solution for genetic diseases. In 1966, Edward Tatum (1909-1975) an American geneticist, published a paper evoking the effectiveness of viruses to be used in somatic-cell genetics and initiating an interest in developing genetic therapy. Of course, at the time this was just an idea, it was a few years later, in 1968, that "proof-of-concept" for virus-mediated gene transfer was generated by Stanfield Rogers and Peter Pfuderer (Wirth, Parker, and Ylä-Herttuala, 2013).

Human Therapeutic Attempts

Steven Rosenberg is an American cancer researcher and surgeon. He received his bachelor's degree and MD from The John Hopkins University and his Ph.D. from Harvard University while completing his residency. The reason for this was that Rosenberg wanted to broaden his scientific knowledge and to better prepare himself for future independent research which he always intended to do, "I wanted to help create the medicine of tomorrow" he claimed (Cavallo, 2018). He most definitely accomplished his goal in 1989, when he conducted the first officially approved gene transfer in humans. Before this, Rogers and Pfuderer performed the first direct human gene therapy trial in the case of two girls suffering from urea cycle disorders. This trial was unsuccessful, however, Rosenberg's trial yielded results indicating seized tumour growth at injection sites and no tumour cells at all after resection and 3 weeks (Wirth, Parker and Ylä-Herttuala, 2013).

It should be noted that in 1990, Martin Cline, an American geneticist, was the first to attempt gene therapy using recombinant DNA, however, he did this without approval from the UCLA Institutional Review Board. This raised efficacy concerns for gene therapy being implemented as a type of therapy, which is why later published papers of Rosenberg are so vital for gene therapy development and implementation as an actual treatment.

Later in 1990, the FDA approved the first ever gene therapy trial in two children suffering from adenosine deaminase deficiency (ADA), a severe condition that leads to immunodeficiency. They were treated by getting their white blood cells extracted from their body, modified to express the normal gene for proper expression. There was an unexpected response and research continued in other parts of the world, as did interest in the field which contributed enormously to gene therapy's development (Wirth, Parker, and Ylä-Herttuala, 2013). However, everything came to a halt in 1999.

The Death Of Jesse Gelsinger

Jesse Gelsinger (1981-1999) suffered from ornithine transcarbamylase, which is an X chromosome-linked disease that affects the liver and hinders the ability to properly break down ammonia. In 1999, Jesse was a participant in a gene therapy clinical trial at the University of Pennsylvania. Unfortunately, the "worst case scenario for gene therapy became a reality". Jesse was injected with an adenoviral vector and died four days later on September 13, 1999, from an immune response caused by the carrying viral vector that led to multiple organ failure and brain death. (Stolberg, 1999). He was the first patient whose death could be directly linked to the viral vector used for the treatment (Wirth, Parker and Ylä-Herttuala, 2013).

This raised a number of concerns surrounding gene therapy and again questioned its ethics. A number of factors like selection of subjects, informed consent, conflict of interest, were strictly overlooked and re-examined. Adults were used with the presumption that they would be able to make better sound decisions and better comprehend the risk of the procedure. Perhaps this was not the best choice. After Jesse's death, the vector used was more closely examined and past research revealed that numerous animals became sick after its use. So, there was a large miscommunication that occurred between the experimenters and also with patients/participants and as a result Jesse was misled. Additionally, there was a conflict of interest identified in the study which contributed to many questioning the ability for sound decisions to be made considering that experimenters had a stake in the outcome ("Gene Therapy Research & the Case of Jesse Gelsinger | NYU Langone Health", 2021).

The FDA suspended the trial stating/citing a failure to train staff adequately, develop basic operating procedures, and obtaining informed consent. Later in 2000, the FDA closely examined other trials involving gene therapy and found that 13 out of 28 needed immediate "remedial action". The FDA and the National Institutes of Health then decided to enhance patient protection by implementing two new programs: The Gene Therapy Clinical Trial Monitoring Plan and the Gene Transfer Safety Symposia (Sibbald, 2001).

Development and Current Position

A lot has changed in the world of gene therapy since the tragic death of Jesse Gelsinger. More research was done, the programs implemented significantly improved the ethical stance of the therapy, and as a result, "gene therapy" was actualized into real practice. In 2003, China became the first country to approve gene therapy-based products for clinical use, and in 2009, the first successful phase III gene therapy trial, in the EU, was achieved. It should be noted that some questions were surrounding China approving this phase III trial, that is to say, not all issues surrounding gene therapy were eliminated following Jesse's death. Despite that, real progress was made.

In 2012, the EMA recommended for the first time a gene therapy product for approval in the EU. This product was Glybera. This product went through multiple approval processes before permission for marketing was authorized. This shows and speaks to the demand for gene therapy medicine from the perspective of the drug itself but also the standards to which they must be held in terms of development. While there are many challenges still associated with gene therapy, the 2012 approval of Glybera demonstrates a giant step forward (Wirth, Parker, and Ylä-Herttuala, 2013).

According to a 2013 paper, cancer is by far the most common disease treated by gene therapy, making up 60% of all ongoing clinical gene therapy trials world-wide. The number of clinical trials at that time was around 1800 (Wirth, Parker, and Ylä-Herttuala, 2013). As of 2017, another journal reports that the number increased to 2597. It can be seen that gene therapy has gradually become more accepted by the government and the public since the 1980s and some of its more controversial and significant missteps (Belete, 2021), but what is even more important is the amount of lives that have been positively impacted due to its further development and all the work that went into making this type of therapy possible.

Conclusion

To conclude, gene therapy along with being a complicated subject also has a complicated history. It is composed of many contributions, small and large, that ultimately led to it being what it is today – a solution to a problem that was once thought to be incurable or unsolvable. A lot of work has been put into improving gene therapy and a lot of work is still required to perfect it. It should also be noted that not everything made it into this chapter, historically, ethically, or factually. This complex subject is growing vastly and already has many parts to it. The goal of this chapter was to focus on some of the major pieces that were significant and may or may not have been discussed in its context before.

Chapter 4: Gene Doping

Chloe Daniva

Introduction

It has seemed to become a trend now where athletes will face the consequences of making headlines for the wrong reasons. To become the most competitive and strongest champion, athletes will go as far as injecting new medicines to upgrade their performance, even to an unfair and secretive advantage. Gene doping (also known as cell doping) is a type of gene therapy that stems from its concept, still in its infancy of science. It is a process in which genetic enhancement occurs in humans through genetic modification. Gene selection can be seen in selective breeding already, however, modifying or replacing genes is a different story. However, the constant research becoming extracted and knowledge being produced make gene therapy no stranger to advancing the system itself. As it is already a known and discussed topic, at least in the sciences, gene therapy involves the injection of foreign DNA into bodies to satisfy the desires of preventing disease or replacing missing genes (John et al., 2020). The term doping originally comes from practice anti-doping agents despise, which is the practice of administering drugs to inhibit or enhance an athlete's performance. This chapter will discuss the present and future blueprint of genetic engineering on gene doping and its current planned application. Of course, it is no surprise that the use of gene therapy is a controversial topic. Organizations like anti-doping agencies challenge the ethics of gene doping in sports. The result of gene doping creates distrust and constant regulations in sport, depending on location. There is much debate as to if the use of genetic modification is fair play, specifically in sports (including nonhuman animal sports, which will be discussed later in this chapter). As ideas of gene doping rapidly advance with the use of the present and thinking towards future technology, the ethics of the process itself must update its regulations as well.

The Upbringing of Gene Doping

Gene therapy is also no stranger to science, however, the upbringing of the specific ideas on gene doping may be new to others. The use of doping begins from the ancient Olympics and includes even the Roman period (Cantelmo et al., 2020). For example, mushroom extracts were used as a substance to enhance sports performance (Cantelmo et al., 2020). Of course, once the knowledge of human genetics had expanded, so did the advancement around the ideas of gene doping. Originally, gene therapy was discovered after the findings used in genetic manipulation, which had been used for humans to battle various types of dangerous diseases (Friedmann, 2010). This rise of events took place approximately in the 1970s and had a huge impact in supporting the birth of gene doping, with genetic engineering officially introducing itself in the 1980s (Friedmann, 2010). Gene manipulation was practiced by changing the amount of enzymes or proteins by increasing or decreasing them in DNA and using genetically modified cells by transferring their polymers (Cantelmo et al., 2020). After this practice had gone through a long and difficult process, including after the Human Genome Project had been initiated, it had still taken additional time to also become regulated and confidently professional in its use (John et al., 2020).

Eventually, gene therapy has officially introduced itself to the sciences and sportspersons. By sportspersons, this could mean the nonhuman and human animal sports industry. By identifying specific genetic traits linked to advantages in athletic performance, gene therapy used in medicine can be applied to the science of gene doping (John et al., 2020). More than 20 polymorphisms have already been proven to present a correlation between athletic performance, sparking growth in future research (John et al., 2020). This method of science could also have stemmed from the artificial gene selection by the selective breeding of nonhuman animals, where gene editing may also occur. Because of newly discussed and potential technologies like CRISPR, there are claims that gene editing can be applied to all organisms (Neuhaus & Parent, 2018). This means the application towards the enhancement of athletic performance in nonhuman animals may also have potential in the sports industry (Neuhaus & Parent, 2018). Traits like strength, being prone to disease and injury, or even just for cosmetic purposes may be achieved with the use of gene editing applications. Of course, this outgrowth of gene therapy is still being researched. The current, future, and ideal applications, due for gene doping, will be discussed in the next section.

Current and Ideal Applications

The use of doping in competitive sports is becoming more popular, especially when it comes to modern day medicine.

However, only the imagination of gene doping has caught the majority of the world because it is still an ongoing discovery in science. Genetic alterations can be made within an athlete's genetic code, enabling the enhancement in an athlete's performance. This can be seen as a way known as "biohacking", as it is compared to a way of "hacking" into the biology set by the genetic code as played by the role of scientists (or in this case, biohackers) (Neuhaus & Parent, 2018). Many genes are being looked into that have a high correlation to the enhancement of athletic performance. These genes provide building blocks for what may inspire the blueprint of gene doping. ACE gene polymorphisms are just one of the "enhancement genes" that are being looked at to be suitable for gene doping (John et al., 2020). As with most clinical applications, there are advantages and disadvantages when it comes to gene doping. There are also possible and fatal consequences that may be faced along the use of gene doping, which can include severe side effects or even malfunctions that can lead to death. As mentioned earlier, gene doping is currently in its early stages regarding modern medicine. Gene doping and its application more commonly attract the attention of elite athletes, who are identified as competitors who compete at a national or international level (John et al., 2020).

Artificial and selective breeding have already been used on nonhuman animals, specifically on animals to be used for sports like cockfighting or bull riding (Neuhaus & Parent, 2018). Scientists and artificial breeders for specifically animal sport, are still in the middle of discovering many other methods to produce the most enhanced "superanimal" (or "superhuman" for human animals) (John et al., 2020). For example, CRISPR is a widely known method that has yet to become fully implanted into the genetic world (Neuhaus & Parent, 2018). CRISPR holds the concept that it is a reliable tool that claims to be able to edit genes in any organism (Neuhaus & Parent, 2018). Methods of gene editing only hold goals to produce the fittest animal in one generation (Neuhaus & Parent, 2018). By "fitness" this could mean advancing traits that are related to the aggressiveness in a rooster for cockfighting, instead of the common method of selective breeding which instead leads to an increase in inhuman deaths (Neuhaus & Parent, 2018).

Ethical Concerns

Most sport agencies maintain regulations to avoid prohibited and uncontrolled use of gene doping (Cantelmo et al., 2020). The ethics of gene doping are constantly up for debate. Sports events have begun to be filled with distrust and constant additions of regulation related to all forms of doping. The World Anti-Doping Agency (WADA) is an organization that regulates methods that can indicate the prohibited practice of doping (John et al., 2020). WADA has currently not been proven to have discovered a method which can indicate athlete's use of gene doping, due to its difficulty in detecting it as it contains such similar characteristics to human proteins (Cantelmo et al., 2020). So far, there has been no evidence of gene doping used in the sporting world (John et al., 2020). However, this does not mean the threat does not await to occur. For the future this means developing new technology that can be approved by the WADA. Fortunately, this can be seen to have a start in its concept of the planning for the Tokyo 2020 Olympics (John et al., 2020).

Another issue regarding gene doping and its concerns with fair play in sport, is the categorization of athletes. Should athletes who have faced genetic manipulation (for the sake of athletic enhancement) be able to play on a team with those who haven't? Or should they compete as an individual with those who also haven't gone through such procedure? What is known as of now with sport is the controversy of segregating sport events by sex chromosomes, the segregation revolving around the Y-chromosome (John et al., 2020). What must now be considered is the categorization between "non-gene-doped" athletes and "gene-doped" athletes, as most may agree with the statement that it would be unfair to merge the two (John et al., 2020). Most would also agree that the threat of gene doping may cause athletes to feel unmotivated to compete against those with unfair advantages and eventually drop out of select competitions, which is not helpful to the sports industry (John et al., 2020).

As mentioned earlier, nonhuman animals are known to face artificial types of breeding. Animal cruelty organizations exist all around the world, however, the ethics about the idea of gene doping these animals appear to lack attention in the media (Neuhaus & Parent, 2018). Using the method of selective breeding is certainly unnatural but it does select and produce desired traits in terms of what scientific breeders deem fittest. However, manipulating the genetic code of these animals is a completely different process, and some may see it as "playing God". Meaning, it is questionable if it is ethical to be taking part in this process. Is it our place to be doing so by affecting the natural process of creation? These nonhuman animals already face the cruelty of being forced by external factors to perform a sport that holds a purpose only to produce a source of entertainment to humans. This industry seems to be cruel to most of the world but unfortunately continues to profit off billions of dollars, being no stranger to the black-market economy (Neuhaus & Parent, 2018). Sadly, the black-market economy is unsurprisingly known to be a major producer that profits from the cruel animal sports industry. This grey area may be the leading cause to its continuous use. Forced events like cockfighting and bull riding continue to happen today around the world, and also continue to put external and unnatural stress on these animals (Neuhaus & Parent, 2018).

Conclusion

Gene doping and its main purpose as an outgrowth of gene therapy are currently due to artificially enhance athletic performance in sports. Instead of replacing or filling in missing genes on the genetic code of an organism, gene doping has the process of inserting whole DNA into an organism's genetic code. With all the uncertainty towards current knowledge on gene doping, the future use of gene doping seems to be further down the line. However, this hopefully provides scientists and the sports world ample time to consider the pros and cons towards the understanding of gene doping. For example, people must be taking into consideration the concept of fairplay in sports or the known and evident harm of nonhuman animals in sport. The ethical concerns on all methods of gene therapy must be discussed before any use. The idea of interfering with natural creation is not a topic taken to be "light" and may not be favorable to all. As well as, the scientific and sports world must not forget that all nonhuman animal lives also matter. Despite all ethical concerns, technology is rapidly advancing and gene editors like CRISPR are already being led by blueprints. It must be noted that inventions like CRISPR stem from science already related to gene therapy between the traditional practices of breeding. Modern technology holds much power to the manipulation and selection of genes already. It is phenomenal how far science has come to the point of birthing an existence to even just the idea of gene doping. The purpose of this article was to bring light and take into consideration the current and future aspects that are sparking conversation through the science of gene doping.

Chapter 5: Clinical Applications of Gene Therapy

Cassandra Van Drunen

Introduction

After years of research, the world is beginning to enter into the era of gene therapy. While earlier chapters have explained what gene therapy exactly is, there are still questions that remain: What can gene therapy be used for and why use it? Ever since the first approved clinical trial for gene therapy in 1988 for the condition known as Gaucher disease, the field, and implementation of gene therapy has grown and spread (Alhankamy et al., 2021). Between 1988 and 2020, there have been more than 46 000 gene therapy clinical trials conducted across the globe (Alhankamy et al., 2021). There are now 3000 genes that have been associated with disease-causing mutations and about 2600 gene therapy trials are currently in progress to manage several disorders (Belete, 2021). As of this year, 16 gene therapy treatments are approved by at least one regulatory authority that can be used for a variety of ailments (Alhankamy et al., 2021). This chapter will explain how gene therapy is currently being used in clinical settings for different ailments in various parts of the world today.

Gene Therapy for Cancer

Across the globe, cancer is the second-highest cause of death in the world, beaten by cardiovascular disease, primarily due to a lack of early diagnosis and the additional high relapse rate of cancer patients (Montaño-Samaniego et al., 2020). It is believed that cancer could surpass cardiovascular disease and become the leading cause of death globally and the World Health Organization has stated that it is estimated that by the year 2030, cancer cases could reach over 20 million across the globe (Montaño-Samaniego et al., 2020). While many other treatment options, including chemotherapy, currently exist, chemotherapeutic drugs are associated with many toxic effects (Montaño-Samaniego et al., 2020). Because of this, a need for new treatment options has persisted, with gene therapy being one of the most promising solutions (Montaño-Samaniego et al., 2020). In fact, gene therapy for cancers represents over 65% of the total clinical trials that have been completed (Alhankamy et al., 2021).

There are some gene therapies currently being used on the market, including Gendicine, Oncorine, and Rexin - G (Alhakamy et al., 2021). Gendicine was first authorized by China in the year 2003 and can be used to treat head and neck squamous cell carcinoma as well as other cancers (Alhankamy et al., 2021). Gendicine was the first gene therapy to be approved worldwide (Frederickson & Ylä-Herttuala, 2019). It is a p53 expressing adenovirus vector that was created by the company known as Shenzhen SiBiono GeneTech Co., Ltd and costs approximately $585 American dollars per dose (Frederickson & Ylä-Herttuala, 2019; Alhankamy et al., 2021). As of 2018, after 12 years of clinical use on over 30 000 patients, Gendicine has been found to have an incredible safety record (Zhang et al., 2018). Additionally, when used alongside traditional chemotherapy and radiation, there have been better response rates in patients than when standard procedures are used

(Zhang et al., 2018). As well, no adverse effects have been reported except for what is known as vector-associated transient fever (Zhang et al., 2018). This condition was present in 50-60% of patients, however, symptoms only lasted for a few short hours (Zhang et al., 2018). The other two aforementioned drugs, Oncorine and Rexin - G, are a genetically modified type five adenovirus used in late-stage refractory nasopharyngeal cancer that was approved in 2005 in China and a retro vector bearing a cytocidal cyclin G1 construct used to treat a range of intractable cancers that was approved in 2007 in the Philippines respectively (Alhankamy et al., 2021).

Gene Therapy for Infectious Diseases

Infectious diseases, most prominently Human Immunodeficiency Virus (HIV) and Hepatitis, account for 3.9% of all clinical trials regarding gene therapy as of 2021, with HIV accounting for 2.8% of the total trials alone (Alhankamy et al., 2021). While progress in antiretroviral therapy has been able to greatly reduce the rate of mortality and increase the quality of life of those that have been infected by HIV since the start of the epidemic around 40 years ago, there are still some challenges with this traditional therapeutic route (Cornu et al., 2021). Factors such as drug resistance, treatment-associated toxicity, the need to adhere to medication guidelines, and the requirement of lifelong therapy are all challenges associated with the current treatment of HIV (Cornu et al., 2021). In the last three decades, there has been substantial progress made in the development of cell and gene therapies for the treatment of HIV (Cornu et al., 2021). Professor Sharon Lewin, the Director of the Doherty Institute of Infection and Immunity at the University of Melbourne believes that gene therapy is more likely to provide the cure for HIV than immunotherapeutic approaches that are aimed at causing long term remission from HIV (Alcorn, 2020). She believes that the proof lies in two HIV patients from Berlin and London, named Timothy Brown and Adam Castellijo, who were both cured of HIV after treatment using stem cell transplants from donors with the CCR5 delta 32 mutation that offers resistance to HIV infected cells (Alcorn, 2020). While there are still many challenges in terms of developing a market ready gene therapy product, such as viral heterogeneity with a singular host, the concept has come a long way over the years (Conru et al., 2021).

There has also been progress in the way of gene therapy treatment for those with Hepatitis. One particular study involving the Chronic Hepatitis B virus (HBV), which affects approximately 257 million individuals globally, has shown some promise (Stone et al., 2020). The Stone et al. team used adeno-associated virus vectors and CRISPR-Staphylococcus aureus (Sa)Cas9 to edit the HBV genome in infected humanized mice subjects. The researchers found the experiment to be successful and believe that with further optimization, their approach could be a way to treat and possibly cure HBV infections (Stone et al., 2020). Overall, while no current gene therapy method exists on the market, the progress made over several decades has become apparent in the scientific community.

Gene Therapy for Primary Immunodeficiencies

The term Primary Immunodeficiencies refers to the heterogeneous group of monogenic conditions that have been determined by either altered immune responses of the adaptive immune system, innate immune system, or both (Cicalese & Aiuti, 2015). There have been over 260 disorders that have been identified that are caused by the mutations in over 300 different genes (Cicalese & Aiuti, 2015). The majority of those suffering from a Primary Immunodeficiency use bone marrow transplantation as their cure (Cicalese & Aiuti, 2015). While survival is excellent with this treatment type, gene therapy has been used successfully for those who were unable to find a suitable donor (Cicalese & Aiuti, 2015). While there has been progress in the field of gene therapy for many Primary Immunodeficiencies, including X-linked SCID (SCID-X1), Wiskott–Aldrich syndrome (WAS), and chronic granulomatous disease (CGD), it is adenosine deaminase (ADA) - SCID that has shown significant advances in terms of gene therapy treatment (Cicalese & Aiuti, 2015).

ADA - SCID is a very rare, inherited autoimmune disease in which patients present with profound lymphopenia as well as impaired development and function of various immune cells including B cells, T cells, and natural killer cells in addition to other non-immunological defects (South et al., 2019). In those with this autoimmune disease, the gene required to make the enzyme ADA is mutated (European Medicines Agency, 2021). Patients with ADA - SCID are usually diagnosed within a year of birth and if left untreated to restore their immune function, will likely die before the age of two (South et al., 2019). ADA - SCID is in fact so rare that in the United Kingdom, it is estimated that of the 20 children who are diagnosed with any type of SCID, there would be 3 or fewer diagnosed with the ADA - SCID subset (South et al., 2019). Back in May of 2016, a drug called Strimvelis was authorized by the EU to be used to treat ADA - SCID (Alhakamy et al., 2021). This drug, which is manufactured by Orchard Therapeutics, costs the equivalent of $648 000 in American money per patient (Alhankamy et al., 2021). Strimvelis uses a sample of a patient's bone marrow so that CD34+ cells, which make lymphocytes, can be extracted from the bone marrow cells (European Medicines Agency, 2021). A properly working gene for ADA is inserted into the CD34+ cell using a retrovirus that has been genetically altered so that it carries the ADA gene into cells but does not cause viral disease in humans (European Medicines Agency, 2021). Once this product is administered to the patient, normal lymphocytes are formed that are able to produce ADA (European Medicines Agency, 2021). This allows patients to better fight infections and overcome the symptoms of ADA - SCID that are related to immune system function (European Medicines Agency, 2021). In one main study of Strimvelis, it was found that all the patients (between the ages of 6 months to 6 years old) were all still alive after 3 years of treatment and that the rate of severe infection decreased after Strimvelis treatment and continued to decline after a 3 year follow up (European Medicines Agency, 2021).

Gene Therapy for Cardiovascular Diseases

As stated in a previous section, cardiovascular diseases, which refers to a wide spectrum of ailments that can be further categorized based on various criteria, are the leading cause of death across the globe (Xu & Song, 2021). Despite this spectrum, if not treated effectively, any of these cardiovascular diseases can lead to heart failure, with effects of 1-2% of the human population, which can lead to a large burden upon society (Xu & Song, 2021). Currently, the main treatment options for most cardiovascular diseases include traditional pharmacotherapy and surgery (Xu & Song, 2021). While these common methods can help to treat the symptoms of various cardiovascular diseases as well as reduce the mortality rate, each has its own set of challenges (Xu & Song, 2021). For example, medications may be beneficial in terms of invasiveness, they can ultimately cause damage to other areas of the body including the liver and kidneys (Xu & Song, 2021). Additionally, while surgery can be a very effective process in terms of treating cardiovascular diseases, these procedures can be complicated and any surgery is subject to potential postoperative complications (Xu & Song, 2021). Due to these reasons, there is a need for a new effective and convenient treatment for cardiovascular diseases, which is why cardiovascular diseases account for 5% of the total amount of clinical gene therapy studies that have occurred (Xu & Song, 2021; Alhankamy et al., 2021).

One research team made interesting developments using Survivin gene therapy (Lee et al., 2014). The study aimed to determine if anti-apoptotic gene therapy through the use of ultrasound-mediated plasmid delivery of Survivin, which is an inhibitor of the apoptosis protein, to prevent apoptosis and attenuate the left ventricular systolic dysfunction of a rat model (Lee et al., 2014). At the end of a six week treatment period, it was concluded that the Survivin therapy was modestly successful (Lee et al., 2014). Another promising gene therapy treatment method for cardiovascular diseases is the augmentation of angiogenesis (Gorabi et al., 2018). It is believed that vascular endothelial growth factor (VEGF) and fibroblast growth factor (FGF) families, hepatocyte growth factor (HGF), as well as gene therapy approaches combined with cell therapy are the most promising contenders for therapeutic vascular growth (Ylä-Herttuala & Baker, 2017).

Conclusion

This chapter has demonstrated that the clinical applications for gene therapy are vast and continue to grow. From current gene therapies that have been approved by various government organizations to the many ongoing clinical trials to create more gene therapies, there is much to talk about in the world of clinical gene therapy. With all the advancements that have occurred over a few short decades, the following years could prove to be fruitful in terms of gene therapy development in various medical fields from cancer to primary immunodeficiencies. By learning from past research, both good implementations and pitfalls, the development of successful, safe, and efficient therapies are sure to develop.

Chapter 6: Social and Ethical Concerns of Gene Therapy

Angelin Valancia Thipahar

Introduction

As discussed in Chapter 1, gene therapy is essentially an experimental technique that uses genes to treat or prevent diseases. The previous chapters have taken you through the general procedure(s) of gene therapy, the different approaches to gene therapy that are being tested by researchers, and the clinical risks involved with this practice. But what is the general perception of gene therapy in society? Is this form of genetic modification a classic example of science gone too far? This section will be addressing these and similar questions. Genetic modification has always carried an air of ethical scrutiny and the complexities of processes related to gene therapy as well as the societal perception of the concept further the debate around whether procedures that involve gene therapy should be permissible. In this chapter, we will be discussing a basic breakdown of the four principled approaches to medical ethics, how the topic of gene therapy relates to these principles, why the topic of genetic modification is a slippery slope, how society views the concept of genetic modification and ethical concerns related to CRISPR biotechnology.

The Four Principle Approach to Medical Ethics: A Brief Overview

One of the methods that researchers and medical professionals have co-opted to assess their treatment methods is the four-principled approach to healthcare ethics. In this approach, there must be consideration to the four principles of beneficence, maleficence, respect for autonomy, and justice. These are prima facie principles, meaning that they are each binding unless they conflict with another principle. Beneficence refers to the moral obligation to 'promote the wellbeing of patients.' Under beneficence, medical practitioners and researchers should do their best to remove or prevent harm from befalling their patients/subjects. The principle of maleficence requires that one abstains from interventions that may cause uncompensated harm to patients or research subjects. Negligent care and providing patients with risky, experimental treatment would be violations of this principle. The principle of autonomy is a requirement to respect the wishes of competent patients and research participants who can decide according to reason. Finally, the principle of justice requires that like cases be treated the same. This principle addresses the right of people to be given necessary treatment regardless of who they are. Now that we have provided a basic ethical framework, let's consider the concept of gene therapy under the guise of this four-principled approach.

Gene Therapy and the Four Principles

Gene therapy is conducted for the well-being of patients. That is the reason that the research and clinical trials are conducted. The ethical issues that surround gene therapy, at least the issues which come to mind for the general public, relate to one of two things: the methods that research practitioners use and the nature of the field as inherently controversial. As you will read about later on in this chapter, there have been times when research has not been properly conducted in this field. Here we will explain what is deemed "proper conduct" for this and, really, any research study.

For any research study involving human participants, there must be informed consent. Consent of this nature must be upfront with the purposes of the research, its expected duration, and the details of the experiments. Any projected risks and benefits of participation should be disclosed. There should be confidentiality with the research records and research-related injuries should be fairly compensated or have proper treatment available. Participants should, ideally, be allowed the right to not participate and withdraw from the study at any point during its duration without penalty (Kapp, 2006). As well as informed consent, the physical and psychological risk to participants should be minimized. Any risk associated with the experiment should be within reason and with consideration of the anticipated benefits. Participants selected for the research should be selected equitably. Now, these are things that can be changed to accommodate modern ethics but the controversy around gene therapy is not similarly subject to change. A large reason why is the concept of the slippery slope argument in relation to gene therapy.

Slippery Slope of Gene Modification

What is a slippery slope argument? Well, the basic structure of a slippery slope can be likened to that of a conditional syllogism. A conditional syllogism, in layman's terms, is a philosophical argument in which if the premise is true, the conclusion must also be true. Similar to this, the slippery slope argument is based on the assumption that if one facet of a controversial topic is permitted, other less ethically ambiguous facets will inevitably become morally permissible. It is best explained through an example. With gene therapy, the slippery slope argument would go as follows: Somatic cell gene therapy will eventually give rise to germline gene therapy. As germline gene therapy is not morally permissible due to the fact that future generations could potentially be harmed through this procedure, we should not allow somatic cell gene therapy (McGleenan, 1995). While it may seem obvious to some of you reading that this argument seems a bit farfetched, this kind of approach is often adopted by the general public when considering morally grey areas of medicine (i.e. gene therapy, abortion, euthanasia, etc.).

In regards to gene therapy, the existence of slippery slope arguments can be traced back to a few sources. Somatic cell gene therapy is widely accepted by most scientists however, the fact that new developments are being cultivated gives rise to the possibility that other forms of gene therapy will one day be permitted. This is particularly frightening to those who have gone through the history of genetics and connected it to that of eugenics. Eugenics is a term that explains the practice of improving the human species by selectively mating people with specific desirable hereditary traits. Some of the historical highlights associated with eugenics include the sterilization of disabled individuals and the Nazi experimentation that occurred throughout World War II. Due to these less than ethical beginnings of genetic medicine, the field has never been wholly trusted. As well, gene therapy is currently only considered for untreatable diseases but, again, this is a topic with a slippery slope. The nature of the illnesses that are treated could change over time. The complexity of the genetic technology and the nature of the procedures as risky only increases the hesitation that people face in regards to genetic medicine. It is important to consider that people will have preconceptions related to gene therapy. Understanding public perceptions of gene therapy is valuable to researchers for several reasons which will be discussed within the following subsection.

How Society Views Gene Therapy and Genetic Modification

In the Beginning: Historical Perspective

Societal perception of gene therapy has had it's ups and downs over the years. An article titled, Gene therapy and the public: a matter of trust assessed the relationship between the society and the concept of gene therapy back in its earlier stages (Gottweis, 2002). The article provided researchers with a better understanding of how general society understood genetic engineering and why, despite the fact that they were able to comprehend various applications of biotechnology, this topic was still controversial. It is important to recognize the fact that prior to testing public knowledge, scientists assumed that public concerns related to gene therapy were founded solely on misunderstanding and lack of scientific information. Through subsequent public opinion studies, it was determined that the public tended to have a generally positive perception of medical biotechnology, and the trepidation associated with gene therapy was founded more on lack of trust, not lack of information.

As Gottweis goes on to say in this article, society has always been somewhat anxious when it comes to this area of science (2002). A large part of the general mistrust of genetic engineering can be attributed to exaggerated beliefs regarding the impact of genetic modification. While the idea that we might cure chronic illnesses using gene-editing mechanisms is a glimmer of hope for those living with these diseases, it does not erase the risks that are associated with these procedures and the air of vague uncertainty that still surrounds them. Any optimism for gene therapy that arises amid the public is quickly extinguished by instances wherein the procedure has gone wrong.

A prime example of this is the death of Jesse Geisinger in 1999 which occurred when the teenager was put through an experimental treatment that subjected the field of gene therapy to immense scrutiny (Rinde, 2019). Jesse suffered from a rare metabolic disorder called ornithine transcarbamylase deficiency syndrome or OTCD. This illness leads to a lethal buildup of ammonia in the blood. While the illness was generally fatal to infants, Jesse had managed to survive to his teenage years by adhering to a careful treatment regime. The clinical trial that Jesse became a part of was aimed at creating a treatment for babies with OTCD. It was meant to be a stepping stone for future treatment and was not done to ameliorate the participants' condition. Nevertheless, Jesse took part in the study and received a modified virus which would infect his liver cells and integrate the added gene into his chromosomal DNA. The virus was altered to be otherwise harmless but, unfortunately, Jesse had a severe reaction to it. Within a day of receiving it, he developed symptoms of jaundice. Shortly afterward he exhibited an intense inflammatory response, developed a dangerous blood-clotting disorder, and experienced kidney, liver and lung failure. Only four days after receiving the treatment, Jesse was declared brain dead. Media coverage of this incident presented the trial researchers as the type that would circumvent a research participant's wellbeing in order to achieve intended results. The Washington Post reported it to be an approach that was moved "too quickly from laboratory bench to the bedside (Weiss & Nelson, 1999)."

The effect of public opinion on gene therapy shocked the science community. Jennifer Doudna, who would go on to discover the CRISPR-Cas9 gene-editing mechanism, remarked that gene therapy was enveloped in taboo pending this tragedy (Rinde, 2019). It got to a point where the field of gene therapy drew such negative connotation that researchers in the field would not want to be referred to as gene therapists. When you consider the gross oversight displayed in human gene therapy research and in Jesse Geisinger's particular case, the blacklisting of the field can be better understood.

Ethical Issues Surrounding the Jesse Gelsinger Case

The largest cause for the societal outrage that followed Jesse Gelsinger's death was the very fact that this teen was, essentially, relatively healthy prior to the clinical trial. Had he not participated in the experiment, he might still have been alive today. A question that was posed in this case was whether the researchers were right to recruit healthy adult volunteers rather than using babies born with OTCD (NYU Langone Health, 2021). The response to this criticism was to point out that informed consent may have been more difficult to attain for the infants. Informed consent is a practice commonly used in the administration of trials, medication and/or procedures. It is the idea that people should be given all necessary information related to their medical situation and the study/procedure at hand before agreeing to it. For young children, parents serve as the decision-makers in consent as children are, generally, not believed capable of ascertaining what is in their best interest. It was assumed, in this case, that parents would not understand that gene therapy experiments were risky procedures that would not serve as miracle cures for their children. Adults with OTCD, on the other hand, would be able to understand the risks and provide their informed consent.

Now this concept of informed consent in relation to this case is not a strong point of opposition to the aforementioned question. Earlier reports showed that past research subjects had become seriously ill as a result of the same vector that caused Jesse Gelsinger's death. This information was not adequately related to Jesse and the other research participants. Jesse's family was similarly not made aware and concluded that Jesse did not know the full extent of the risk he was undertaking. By allowing Jesse Gelsinger to participate in this experiment without giving him all the necessary information, the researchers violated the principle of beneficence as they acted in a manner which led to harm. Now this, by itself, is unethical but unfortunately, the lapse in moral judgement does not end there. James Wilson, the director of the University of Pennsylvania's Institute for Human Gene Therapy, was involved in this trial and was accused of a conflict of interest with this research. It was discovered that Wilson had shares in the company that owned the gene-transfer technology which meant that, had the trial succeeded, he stood to gain a massive sum. While Wilson's claims that Jesse's reaction was an unpredictable error could not be outright refuted, the FDA suspended human research at UPenn's Institute for Human Gene Therapy in early 2000 and the program itself was shut down as well (Rinde, 2019).

Looking Forward: Current Public Opinion

While the field has regained its credibility in the decades following this incident, the question of whether or not current gene-therapy research is safer is ongoing. In a more recent systematic review regarding public opinions of gene therapy, perceptions of the concept, especially for medical reasons and chronic/fatal diseases, were positive (Delhove et al., 2020). The review assessed beliefs and attitudes toward gene therapy and gene editing for human use. It also highlighted factors that influenced the acceptability of the field which is essential for research to continue in a progressive manner as it will encourage positive perception of future clinical trials.
In general, gene therapies involving somatic cells were observed to have higher levels of acceptability than germline therapies. This is likely due to the fact that, while the former is generally contained to a single patient, the latter can be passed onto future generations (Memi et al., 2018). Monogenic inherited disorders where the mutations in a single gene cause disease are those which are most applicable for gene therapy and gene editing. Gene therapy is typically meant to target rare illnesses that do not have alternative treatment methods and are associated with premature death. The existence of these genetic modification strategies offers significant hope for people with these illnesses but, as seen from the Jesse Gelsinger case, the potential risks associated with the delivery process of the treatment as well as the fact that there may be permanent changes to the host cell genome is cause for

concern. Gene vector designs have been improved significantly in the last two decades. Severe reactions to treatments are better understood and much less likely to occur today. This is not to say that risks are not present and, indeed, it is hard for researchers to glean the full extent of the risk associated with gene therapy.

Current public opinion regarding gene therapy has not diverged from historical opinion in any extreme way. Conversations around gene therapy and gene-editing are still made with hopeful tones however, any clinical trials conducted without appropriate consideration of their subjects will undoubtedly lead to a decline in societal perception of the field. To put it simply, the idea behind gene therapy has been generally accepted but it is a field under a massive amount of scrutiny which means that social concerns will never really diminish. Regardless of the social and ethical concerns revolving around the field of gene therapy, it is a field that is necessary for the better understanding of chronic illnesses and the development of more suitable treatments for individuals living with these diseases.

Chapter 7: Future Directions of Gene Therapy

Sahir Dhalla

Gene therapy was a discovery that revolutionized the biomedical industry. It opened up a new world of biotechnology and advanced therapy methods that have the potential to treat an immense number of previously incurable illnesses. The likes of cancer, cystic fibrosis, and diabetes are some of the most prominent ones that, previously, only ever had hopes of being mitigated and reduced, whereas now they have the potential to be cured. It is perhaps the fastest-growing field in medicine at the moment, and the trend looks likely to continue, with the field reaching new heights in advanced therapies and allowing medical professionals to cure even more ailments. But the field and treatments are not without fault. There are a considerable number of issues that already impact the field, and there will be a great number more to face as the field develops into a more commonplace treatment.

Future of Gene Therapy in Medicine

Ever since gene therapy became well-known in the scientific community, it was regarded as something that had the potential to treat devastating inherited diseases for which we have no cure, and for which there is not much hope of finding a conventional cure (Cavazzana-Calvo et al., 2014). Already, even in this short frame of time, gene therapy has shown promise in treating a variety of previously incurable diseases, including the likes of cancer, cystic fibrosis, heart disease, diabetes, hemophilia, and AIDS. However, these are only currently done as clinical trials and are not always available or safe for the general public. As the field develops further, researchers and medical professionals will look towards making these treatments more accessible, as well as more effective and reliable at treating these illnesses and far more.

Cancer, for example, has seen massive changes in the field of gene therapy and other treatments over the past two decades. These changes have come in the form of new and improved delivery methods for the treatments - methods that reduce certain risks and can carry out a far more diverse range of tasks than was previously possible (El-Aneed, 2004; Amer, 2014). Issues such as leukemia symptoms arising in patients and severe immune responses have been curbed massively, promoting gene therapy trials across the world and increasing the pace at which the field develops. And, considering the rapid rate we are witnessing in the field, it would not be too far-fetched to suggest that issues reported within the past few years will be reduced or maybe even eliminated within the next decade or two. These include some milder issues like flu symptoms, but also some more worrying issues such as toxicity and immunogenicity - the ability of a foreign substance to evoke an immune response (Amer, 2014).

All the treatments and trials so far have been focused on finding cures that help issues that were previously considered incurable, but that isn't the only area gene therapies could benefit from. Considering the genetic basis for most diseases, it would be just as interesting to consider the use of gene therapies in conventional issues that generally use drug therapies. While the current focus of gene therapy is high-risk and terminal patients for whom conventional treatments are not useful, there is nothing to say that gene therapies cannot find their future within the context of drug therapies too (McCain, 2005). There will eventually be a point at which gene therapy and conventional medicine will overlap. It is at this point that gene therapy will become a far more beneficial tool, reaching its abilities past chronic life-threatening illnesses and helping with other acute or chronic issues that affect the general public.

But while gene therapy is an incredible achievement and has not fulfilled its potential yet, medical professionals also need to be mindful of using it as a one-size-fits-all type of treatment. A study by Shapiro et al. (2018) suggests further studies into predictive systems for the need for gene therapy alongside studies into gene therapies themselves. Ideally, these systems would be personalized to each patient and their issues and would be able to suggest safer and more cost-effective approaches and would be especially vital in cases where gene therapy has adverse impacts.

Overall, the future of gene therapy in all areas of medicine looks bright but must be applied more carefully. Gene therapy has the potential to be able to cure and help any number of diseases and conditions, both those that are presently known and those that may be discovered in the future, especially when considering the immense number of conventional issues that also have a genetic basis. But we must be wary of applying this miraculous treatment to every condition that arises. Due to issues that are unique to each person and their immune systems, gene therapy treatments may not be suitable to everyone, as effective as they may be, so there will need to be measures and systems in place to ensure patient safety in all cases.

Gene Editing

CRISPR is a term that has dominated biomedical journal and magazine headlines for the past few years, and with good reason too. CRISPR-Cas9 is a new technology that is simple in its implementation but with extremely powerful consequences. It allows researchers to easily change and alter DNA sequences by removing, adding, or altering certain parts of the genome in any creature. Though not without risk, it has a thoroughly promising future in gene therapy treatments, allowing for even some changes from birth that could lead to better immunity, strength, or other characteristics for the child in the future.

It is perhaps the field of gene therapy that has shown the greatest ethical consequences, and yet the most rapid evolution and route for treatment. CRISPR-Cas9 is essentially a technology that would allow researchers to alter DNA of any kind, from simple changes in animals to things like eye colour or hair colour and other inherited traits. Immunity is probably the most intriguing one at the moment in the context of gene therapies. Because of the genetic basis of so many diseases and the impact each individual's unique immune system has on the ability of a disease such as HIV to affect them, gene editing is being considered as a method for altering one's immune system from birth to develop better immunity for this. Obviously, in cases of HIV, there are far safer methods so these dire issues are not necessary, but there are other diseases for which gene editing could be a revolutionary, albeit ethically ambiguous, method for getting rid of them. The main concern, however, remains that we don't know enough about the consequences for gene editing. When Chinese researcher He Jiankui first tested this technology on embryos, he received immediate and thorough backlash for his actions because, simply put, no one could predict the long-term impacts of that treatment, and it was exceedingly unethical to have done that (Rosenbaum, 2019).

While the future of CRISPR-Cas9 is unclear, its potential is virtually unlimited and can have major implications for the future of gene therapy and the broader medical field too. In fact, its implications seem so dangerous that Jennifer Doudana, a biochemist whose research led to this gene-editing technique, noted in her memoir that she had nightmares where a pig-faced Hitler summons her and asks her to describe the implementation and potential implications of the technology she developed (Doudna & Sternberg, 2018). And these issues don't just plague her when she is asleep. She warns against reckless endeavours with the CRISPR technology, claiming that "through a series of reckless, poorly conceived experiments, scientists would prematurely implement CRISPR without proper oversight or consideration of the risks." And it is unfortunate that her warnings have proven to be true numerous times in just the past few years already.

Potential Concerns Within the Field

As with every field of science and medicine, gene therapy and editing are not perfect as they are and will need some notable changes to continue growing. Probably the most significant one of these, as mentioned earlier, is the issue that some treatments still have with toxicity and immunogenicity. In some contemporary gene therapy trials, several delivery methods used in gene therapy such as pseudotyped retroviruses and lentiviruses have shown to be toxic to certain primary cells (McCain, 2005). This sort of reaction can be extremely costly and dangerous to patients, and so the field has worked to curb issues like this that arise.

These issues do, however, create an interesting situation where one health issue is almost 'traded' for another (Cavazzana-Calvo et al., 2014). The potential trade-off when using these gene therapies on at-risk patients is that they may end up with certain symptoms of other life-threatening ailments, but their current actually life-threatening illness is cured or reduced enough to no longer be life-threatening. This is something that needs to again be considered from patient to patient, assessing the risks that will come with doing the gene therapy treatments and whether it will be worth it. As touched on earlier, it would be worth investing into research that creates better systems for understanding each patient's unique genetic makeup and how they might react to the treatments to make better decisions about whether to provide them or not.

A great deal of work is already being done to work on issues like immunogenicity when it comes to particular types of gene therapy treatments. Already, researchers have tested a variety of methods, many with promising results that show no detectable immunogenicity (Finn et al., 2012). These methods also have shown far less toxicity all throughout the system and the body. Considering this trend and the immense pace of the research that occurs in gene therapy, it is evident that these issues will eventually be reduced to a near unimportant risk when gene therapies can be administered to the general public for conditions.

Besides the issues that can be sorted with increased research and time spent in this field, there are certain issues that arise as a result of the quality and planning of clinical trials, as opposed to the drugs that are being developed and tested. An article on gene therapy trials for cancer found that the "lack of success in many trials is due to patient selection" (Amer, 2014). Because of genetic variations between individuals, each person and their immune systems may respond differently to the application of the same gene therapies, leading to results with less reproducibility and reliability. Certain therapies that are deemed unsafe, maybe, might only have been so because of the patient's unique disposition towards a certain treatment and could be found to be solidly reliable in other trials. Some recommend the use of better patient and tumour genetic analysis systems, as well as a better understanding of the host's cellular immunity to facilitate better trials and appropriate gene therapies for each patient.

Rising External Concerns

No matter how incredible or revolutionary gene therapy gets though, there will be strong external concerns that will arise from outside the field that will have to be faced. From issues like economic backing to those of policy or ethical concerns, the field will face a large change over the next decades as it evolves in the context of the wider medical market. Studies themselves will have hurdles and issues of their own, having to overcome differing gene therapy treatments and stringent regulations that could hamper the rate of development for gene therapies, for better or for worse.

The first category of these issues is regulatory and economic issues. It is the sad truth of many countries today that to get anywhere in academia, a lab or group of researchers need funding, and this is especially the case with gene therapy. Gene therapy is, on its own, an extremely expensive field, with most modern therapies costing upwards of $5 billion to develop and implement, accounting for labs, researchers, manufacturing, distribution, and the immensely stringent regulatory pathways before they can be used (Irvine, 2019). This high cost not only makes it difficult for smaller labs and groups from being able to develop these therapies, but it also often acts as a deterrent for other pharmaceutical companies to invest in it. But this is one trend that might change. As gene therapies further enter the limelight, it is becoming immensely clear that they are the future of medicine, especially in cases of currently untreatable diseases, and there is a large market opportunity here that companies may be interested in investing in.

Alternatively, government funding is a factor that must be considered. Medicine in gene therapy, especially for chronic life-threatening illnesses, is becoming more and more a concern for public health, especially as populations age across the globe. As gene therapy becomes more applicable to the general public, it would make sense to divert a larger amount of public funding towards gene therapy research and development, especially when considering the immense potential it has to cure diseases and ailments. In parts of the world that would benefit most from gene therapy, such as those in Africa, academics are already highlighting the lack of direct public funding as a reason for the stagnating research being conducted in the field (Arbuthnot et al., 2017).

These economic challenges in conjunction with certain regulatory and scientific issues also face those who aim to take these clinical trials and studies and apply them properly in medical practices. A review by Shapiro et al. (2018) focuses on the field of osteogenesis and points out that, although more and more strategies are being created for the application of gene therapy, it is becoming increasingly difficult to figure out which ones should actually be elevated to clinical trials.

From a scientific perspective, this issue occurs because of the disparity between gene therapies and the reactions to them. Whatever applies to one creature that a therapy has been tested on may not apply to another, and while comparative studies can be drawn, they are potentially incorrect when actually tested. Studies that can overcome this issue along with regulatory and economic issues will also have another concern to address - the immense range of gene therapies that can be applied to a single illness. Because of the way gene therapy works, it cannot be a one size fits all kind of treatment, and so many of them will need to be thoroughly researched and developed.

Certain semantics and smaller issues will also need to be addressed and properly implemented into policies once gene therapy becomes more commonplace. An example of such an area that will require additional guidelines is that of blood donation. Certain policies that indirectly address this issue already exist, such as policies that prevent individuals who have had cancer from donating blood for a certain lengthy period of time after their treatment, but these guidelines don't apply to all avenues that gene therapy reaches into. Since we still aren't fully aware of the long-term impacts that gene therapy has on one's blood and functions, it would not be safe to permit individuals who have undergone gene therapy to donate blood, so new guidelines and policies would need to be implemented. This is one of a few categories where such guidelines may be required.

Impact of Current Policies on the Future

Probably the biggest obstacle facing gene therapy, aside from funding, is regulatory bodies and certain policies that impede the rate of advancement in the field, despite their original intentions. While the use of policies to regulate scientific endeavours is useful in maintaining a higher standard and safety level of experiments and clinical trials — especially for certain morally ambiguous proposed trials — many of the requirements are often prohibitive for researchers and medical professionals. And this impact is marked heavily in the gene therapy research and development processes.

A rather extreme example of policies with good intentions impeding the progress in this field can be seen in the late 1990s to early 2000s. During that period, some countries put a full hold on studies in gene therapy, particularly those that involved the use of retroviruses (Cavazzana-Calvo et al., 2014). In some countries such as the United Kingdom, clinical trials were never put on hold, but treating patients was prohibited even in life-threatening cases. It took until 2003 for other countries in Europe to allow patient treatments, and even then it was only in extreme life-threatening cases that took a lot of approval for use. These issues have had their impact even until the past few years, throwing the field into a recession as a combination of all the scepticism, bad press, and responses from regulatory bodies. If this sort of trend continues, the field will struggle to ever develop fully applicable treatments for diseases, both life-threatening ones and other chronic issues.

Important and beneficial steps have already been taken though when it comes to outdated policies. Gene therapies and other new forms of treatments have been classified in the European Union as advanced therapy medicinal products (ATMPs) with its own regulatory committee and sets of policies that apply to these products (Terai & Suda, 2016). Having a separate committee is something that should be adopted in the future by other regional policy groups when it comes to advanced medicines such as gene therapies and any others that come along in the future as it allows for more appropriate measures and better coverage of these therapies and doesn't impact the current policies that work for other conventional measures. A book by Terai and Suda (2016) went over current policies and gave a few suggestions as to how these issues should be handled in the future. A first place where great considerations must be made is with regards to the rights of the donor. Certain rights such as privacy and decision making with regards to the pluripotent stem cells that are donated must be respected greatly and kept in mind when designing guidelines and policies. The dignity of life is also a point stressed in the book. Protecting this dignity of life is not only a morally correct method of acting, but it also works to expedite the process of clinical application from scientific experimentation.

It is clear that the future of gene therapy is a bright one. The field is riddled with promise and has immense potential in treating a whole number of diseases. However, we must proceed with caution and deliberation, because a few reckless steps could spell disaster not just for the field, but for the future of medicine in general. Those in charge of policies and regulations must be mindful of the impacts they are having on the future of science, while medical professionals and researchers must ensure they do not work too hastily, implementing procedures and treatments that are rushed and nowhere near as complete as they could be. Gene therapy has revolutionized the present, but it must work just as hard to revolutionize the future.

Conclusion

Gene therapy was considered revolutionary when first discovered, and is starting to make its mark on science and society today. While many questions about its practicality and usage remain, the wide range of clinical applications, from cancer to heart disease, cannot be understated. With new and exciting developments in this field occurring all the time, the future of this technology is truly limitless and is projected to bring about a fundamental change to how we address disease in the future.

References

Chapter 1

Carmichael, L. E. (2014). Gene Therapy. *Essential Library.* http://ezproxy.macewan.ca/login?url=https://search.ebscohost.com/login.aspx?direct=true&db=nlebk&AN=609188&site=eds-live&scope=site&ebv=EB&ppid=pp_8

Cotrim, A. P., & Baum, B. J. (2008). Gene Therapy: Some History, Applications, Problems, and Prospects. Toxicologic Pathology, 36(1), 97–103. https://doi.org/10.1177/0192623307309925

Dickler, H. B., & Collier, E. (1994). Gene therapy in the treatment of disease. The Journal of Allergy and Clinical Immunology, 94(6 Part 1 Suppl), 942–951. https://doi.org/10.1016/0091-6749(94)90111-2

Rangel Gonçalves, G. A., & de Melo Alves Paiva, R. (2017). Gene therapy: advances, challenges and perspectives. *Einstein, 15*(3), 369–375. https://doi.org/10.1590/S1679-45082017RB4024

Scheller, E. L., & Krebsbach, P. H. (2009). Gene therapy: design and prospects for craniofacial regeneration. Journal of Dental Research, 88(7), 585–596. https://doi.org/10.1177/0022034509337480

U.S. Food & Drug Administration. (2017). What is Gene Therapy? How Does It Work? https://www.fda.gov/consumers/consumer-updates/what-gene-therapy-how-does-it-work

Wirth, T., Parker, N., & Ylä-Herttuala, S. (2013). History of gene therapy. Gene, 525(2), 162–169. https://doi.org/10.1016/j.gene.2013.03.137

Chapter 2

Beutler, E. (2001). The cline affair. *Molecular Therapy, 4*(5), 396–397. https://doi.org/10.1006/mthe.2001.0486

Friedmann, T. (1992). A brief history of gene therapy. *Nature Genetics, 2*(2), 93–98. https://doi.org/10.1038/ng1092-93

Gonçalves, G. A. R., & Paiva, R. de M. A. (2017). Gene therapy: Advances, challenges and perspectives. *Einstein, 15*(3), 369–375. https://doi.org/10.1590/S1679-45082017RB4024

Helper Cell—An overview | *ScienceDirect Topics.* (n.d.). Retrieved July 30, 2021, from https://www.sciencedirect.com/topics/medicine-and-dentistry/helper-cell

Koo, B. C., Kwon, M. S., & Kim, T. (2014). 6—Retrovirus-Mediated Gene Transfer. Transgenic Animal Technology (Third Edition) (pp. 167–194). Elsevier. https://doi.org/10.1016/B978-0-12-410490-7.00006-2

Mitha, F. (2020, November 4). The Return of Gene Therapy: A Historical Overview. *Labiotech.Eu.* https://www.labiotech.eu/in-depth/gene-therapy-history/

Scollay, R. (2001). Gene Therapy. A Brief Overview of the Past, Present, and Future. *Annals of the New York Academy of Sciences, 953a*(1 NEW VISTAS IN), 26–30. https://doi.org/10.1111/j.1749-6632.2001.tb11357.x

What is gene therapy? (2021). MedlinePlus Genetics. Retrieved July 26, 2021, from https://medlineplus.gov/genetics/understanding/therapy/genetherapy/

Wirth, T., Parker, N., & Ylä-Herttuala, S. (2013). History of gene therapy. *Gene, 525*(2), 162–169. https://doi.org/10.1016/j.gene.2013.03.137

Chapter 3

Altman, L. (2005). *Maclyn McCarty Dies at 93; Pioneer in DNA Research.* New York Times.

Bansal, M. (2003). DNA structure: Revisiting the Watson–Crick double helix. *Current Science, 85*(11), 1556-1563. Retrieved July 30, 2021, from http://www.jstor.org/stable/24110017

Belete, T. (2021). The Current Status of Gene Therapy for the Treatment of Cancer. *Biologics: Targets And Therapy, Volume 15,* 67-77. doi: 10.2147/btt.s302095

Britannica, T. Editors of Encyclopaedia (2021, January 1). Frederick Griffith. Encyclopedia Britannica. https://www.britannica.com/biography/Frederick-Griffith

Cavallo, J. (2018). Steven A. Rosenberg Works to Unmask Cancer's Achilles Heel - The ASCO Post. Retrieved 31 July 2021, from https://ascopost.com/issues/november-25-2018/steven-a-rosenberg-works-to-unmask-cancer-s-achilles-heel/

E.L. Tatum, J. Lederberg(1947). *Gene Recombination in the Bacterium Escherichia coli J. Bacteriol.*, 53 pp. 673-684

Gene Therapy Research & the Case of Jesse Gelsinger | NYU Langone Health. (2021). Retrieved 31 July 2021, from https://med.nyu.edu/departments-institutes/population-health/divisions-sections-centers/medical-ethics/education/high-school-bioethics-project/learning-scenarios/jesse-gelsinger-case

Harman, Oren S., and Michael R. Dietrich. Rebels, Mavericks, and Heretics in Biology. New Haven: Yale UP, 2009. Print.

Maddox, B. (2003). The double helix and the 'wronged heroine'. *Nature, 421*(6921), 407-408. doi: 10.1038/nature01399

Sambrook, J., Westphal, H., Srinivasan, P., & Dulbecco, R. (1968). The integrated state of viral DNA in SV40-transformed cells. *Proceedings Of The National Academy Of Sciences, 60*(4), 1288-1295. doi: 10.1073/pnas.60.4.1288

Sibbald B. (2001). Death but one unintended consequence of gene-therapy trial. *CMAJ : Canadian Medical Association journal = journal de l'Association medicale canadienne, 164*(11), 1612.

Stolberg, S. (1999). *The Biotech Death of Jesse Gelsinger. The New York Times Magazine.*

Zinder, N.D., Lederberg, J (1952). *Genetic exchange in Salmonella J. Bacteriol.*, 64 pp. 679-699

Chapter 4

Cantelmo, R. A., Da Silva, A. P., Mendes-Junior, C. T., & Dorta, D. J. (2020). Gene doping: Present and future. *European journal of sport science, 20*(8), 1093-1101. https://www.researchgate.net/publication/337658051_Gene_doping_Present_and_future

Friedmann, T. (2010). How close are we to gene doping?. The Hastings Center Report, 20-22. https://doi.org/10.1353/hcr.0.0246

John, R., Dhillon, M. S., & Dhillon, S. (2020). Genetics and the elite athlete: our understanding in 2020. *Indian journal of orthopaedics, 54*(3), 256-263. https://doi.org/10.1007/s43465-020-00056-z

Neuhaus, C. P., & Parent, B. (2019). Gene Doping—in Animals? Ethical Issues at the Intersection of Animal Use, Gene Editing, and Sports Ethics. *Cambridge Quarterly of Healthcare Ethics, 28*(1), 26-39. doi:10.1017/S096318011800035X

Chapter 5

Alcorn, K. (2020). *Gene therapy or immunotherapy: which approach is more likely to deliver a cure for HIV?*. Retrieved 28 July 2021, from https://www.aidsmap.com/news/jul-2020/gene-therapy-or-immunotherapy-which-approach-more-likely-deliver-cure-hiv

Alhakamy, N. A., Curiel, D. T., & Berkland, C. J. (2021). The era of gene therapy: From preclinical development to clinical application. *Drug Discovery Today.* https://doi.org/10.1016/j.drudis.2021.03.021

Belete, T. M. (2021). The Current Status of Gene Therapy for the Treatment of Cancer. *Biologics, 15,* 67–77. https://doi.org/10.2147/BTT.S302095

Cicalese, M. P., & Aiuti, A. (2015). Clinical Applications of Gene Therapy for Primary Immunodeficiencies. *Human Gene Therapy, 26*(4), 21–219. https://doi.org/10.1089/hum.2015.047

Cornu, T., Mussolino, C., Müller, M., Wehr, C., Kern, W., & Cathomen, T. (2021). HIV Gene Therapy: An Update. *Human Gene Therapy, 32*(1-2), 52-65. doi: 10.1089/hum.2020.159

European Medicines Agency (2021). *Strimvelis.* Retrieved 28 July 2021, from https://www.ema.europa.eu/en/medicines/human/EPAR/strimvelis

Frederickson, R. M., & Ylä-Herttuala, S. (2019). Two Decades of Molecular Therapy: The Journey Continues. *Molecular Therapy, 27*(1), 1–2. https://doi.org/10.1016/j.ymthe.2018.12.004

Gorabi, A. M., Hajighasemi, S., Tafti, H. A., Soleimani, M., Panahi, Y., Ganjali, S., & Sahebkar, A. (2018). Gene therapy in cardiovascular diseases: A review of recent updates. *Journal of Cellular Biochemistry, 119*(12), 9645–9654. https://doi.org/10.1002/jcb.27303

Lee, P. J. H., Rudenko, D., Kuliszewski, M. A., Liao, C., Kabir, M. G., Connelly, K. A., & Leong-Poi, H. (2014). Survivin gene therapy attenuates left ventricular systolic dysfunction in doxorubicin cardiomyopathy by reducing apoptosis and fibrosis. *Cardiovascular Research, 101*(3), 423–433. https://doi.org/10.1093/cvr/cvu001

Montaño-Samaniego, M., Bravo-Estupiñan, D. M., Méndez-Guerrero, O., Alarcón-Hernández, E., & Ibáñez-Hernández, M. (2020). Strategies for Targeting Gene Therapy in Cancer Cells With Tumor-Specific Promoters. *Frontiers in Oncology, 10*, 605380–605380. https://doi.org/10.3389/fonc.2020.605380

South, E., Cox, E., Meader, N., Woolacott, N., & Griffin, S. (2019). Strimvelis ® for Treating Severe Combined Immunodeficiency Caused by Adenosine Deaminase Deficiency: An Evidence Review Group Perspective of a NICE Highly Specialised Technology Evaluation. *PharmacoEconomics - Open, 3*(2), 151–161. https://doi.org/10.1007/s41669-018-0102-3

Xu, M., & Song, J. (2021). Targeted Therapy in Cardiovascular Disease: A Precision Therapy Era. *Frontiers in Pharmacology, 12,* 623674–623674. https://doi.org/10.3389/fphar.2021.623674

Ylä-Herttuala, S., & Baker, A. H. (2017). Cardiovascular Gene Therapy: Past, Present, and Future. *Molecular Therapy, 25*(5), 1095–1106. https://doi.org/10.1016/j.ymthe.2017.03.027

Zhang, W., Li, L., Li, D., Liu, J., Li, X., & Li, W. et al. (2018). The First Approved Gene Therapy Product for Cancer Ad-p53(Gendicine): 12 Years in the Clinic. *Human Gene Therapy, 29*(2), 160-179. doi: 10.1089/hum.2017.218

Chapter 6

Delhove, J., Osenk, I., Prichard, I., & Donnelley, M. (2020). Public acceptability of gene therapy and gene editing for human use: A systematic review. *Human Gene Therapy, 31*(1-2), 20–46. https://doi.org/10.1089/hum.2019.197

Gene therapy research & the case of Jesse Gelsinger. NYU Langone Health. (n.d.). https://med.nyu.edu/departments-institutes/population-health/divisions-sections-centers/medical-ethics/education/high-school-bioethics-project/learning-scenarios/jesse-gelsinger-case.

Gottweis, H. (2002). Gene therapy and the public: A matter of trust. *Gene Therapy, 9*(11), 667–669. https://doi.org/10.1038/sj.gt.3301752

Kapp, M. B. (2006). Ethical and legal issues in research involving human subjects: Do you want a piece of me? *Journal of Clinical Pathology, 59*(4), 335–339. https://doi.org/10.1136/jcp.2005.030957

McGleenan, T. (1995). Human gene therapy and slippery slope arguments. *Journal of Medical Ethics, 21*(6), 350–355. https://doi.org/10.1136/jme.21.6.350

Memi, F., Ntokou, A., & Papangeli, I. (2018). CRISPR/Cas9 gene-editing: RESEARCH technologies, clinical applications and ethical considerations. *Seminars in Perinatology, 42*(8), 487–500. https://doi.org/10.1053/j.semperi.2018.09.003

Rinde, M. (2019, July 16). *The death of Jesse GELSINGER, 20 years later.* Science History Institute. https://www.sciencehistory.org/distillations/the-death-of-jesse-gelsinger-20-years-later.

Weiss, R., & Nelson, D. (1999, September 29). *Teen Dies Undergoing Experimental Gene Therapy.* The Washington Post. https://www.washingtonpost.com/wp-srv/WPcap/1999-09/29/060r-092999-idx.html.

Chapter 7

Amer, M. H. (2014). Gene therapy for cancer: present status and future perspective. *Molecular and Cellular Therapies, 2*(1), 27–27. https://doi.org/10.1186/2052-8426-2-27

Arbuthnot, P., Maepa, M. B., Ely, A., & Pepper, M. S. (2017). The state of gene therapy research in Africa, its significance and implications for the future. *Gene Therapy, 24*(9), 581–589. https://doi.org/10.1038/gt.2017.57

Cavazzana-Calvo, M., Mavilio, F., & Thrasher, A. (2004). The future of gene therapy. *Nature, 427*(6977), 779–781. https://doi.org/10.1038/427779a

Doudna, J. A., Sternberg, S. H. (2018). *A crack in creation: gene editing and the unthinkable power to control human evolution.* New York: Houghton Mifflin Harcourt Publishing.

El-Aneed, A. (2004). An overview of current delivery systems in cancer gene therapy. *Journal of Controlled Release, 94*(1), 1–14. https://doi.org/10.1016/j.jconrel.2003.09.013

Finn, J. D., Nichols, T. C., Svoronos, N., Merricks, E. P., Bellenger, D. A., Zhou, S., Simioni, P., High, K. A., & Arruda, V. R. (2012). The efficacy and the risk of immunogenicity of FIX Padua (R338L) in hemophilia B dogs treated by AAV muscle gene therapy. *Blood, 120*(23), 4521–4523. https://doi.org/10.1182/blood-2012-06-440123

McCain J. (2005). The future of gene therapy. *Biotechnology healthcare, 2*(3), 52–60.

Rosenbaum, L. (2019). The Future of Gene Editing — Toward Scientific and Social Consensus. *The New England Journal of Medicine, 380*(10), 971–975. https://doi.org/10.1056/NEJMms1817082

Shapiro, G., Lieber, R., Gazit, D., & Pelled, G. (2018). Recent Advances and Future of Gene Therapy for Bone Regeneration. *Current Osteoporosis Reports, 16*(4), 504–511. https://doi.org/10.1007/s11914-018-0459-3

Terai, S., & Suda, T. (2016). *Gene Therapy and Cell Therapy Through the Liver Current Aspects and Future Prospects* (1st ed. 2016.). Springer Japan. https://doi.org/10.1007/978-4-431-55666-4